BANNEKER
THE AFRO-AMERICAN ASTRONOMER

BANNEKER
THE AFRO-AMERICAN ASTRONOMER

WILL W. ALLEN
and DANIEL MURRAY

Black Classic Press

Baltimore

BANNEKER
THE AFRO-AMERICAN ASTRONOMER

Copyright 1921
by Will W. Allen

First published 1921

Published 2005
by Black Classic Press

All Rights Reserved.

Library of Congress Card Catalog Number: 96-084733

ISBN 0-933121-48-2

Cover design by Michelle D. Wright

Printed by BCP Digital
An affiliate company of Black Classic Press

Founded in 1978, Black Classic Press specializes in bringing to light obscure
and significant works by and about people of African descent. If our books are
not available in your area, ask your local bookseller to order them.

You can purchase books and obtain a list of our titles from:

Black Classic Press
c/o List
P.O. Box 13414
Baltimore, MD 21203
Also visit:
www.blackclassic.com

BENJAMIN BANNEKER

CONTENTS

INTRODUCTION

THE author, or to be more precise, the compiler of this work, while in Maryland, found in the house of Samuel H. Hopkins, of Howard county, a copy of a letter written by one Benjamin Banneker to Thomas Jefferson, Secretary of State.

He became interested on account of the beautiful language of this colored man's letter written in 1792, and at that time no doubt, Banneker was with a few exceptions the only colored man south of the Mason and Dixon Line who could read and write beyond the ordinary.

The compiler became enthused and started to find out all he could about this remarkable man. He deems it his duty to publish his findings and to place a copy in the home of every colored family in the United States.

Credit is given herein to:

Martha E. Tyson papers, compiled by her daughter, Anne T. Kirk.

INTRODUCTION

Daniel Murray, an Assistant Librarian of the Library of Congress.

P. Lee Phillip, Esq., of the Columbia Historical Society.

Henry Proctor Slaughter, editor Odd Fellows Journal.

Henry E. Baker, in the Journal of Negro History.

And to the Maryland Historical Society.

Feeling that the memory of this colored astronomer should be kept green, I place the accompanying facts in the hands of the public.

WILL W. ALLEN.

September 15, 1921.

A PAPER

Read Before the BANNEKER ASSOCIATION OF WASHINGTON *by* DANIEL MURRAY, *an Assistant Librarian of the Library of Congress.*

My Friends:

I am particularly gratified over the opportunity afforded me to recall to the attention of the living the virtues and intellectual powers of one of the illustrious dead. And it is all the more gratifying since your assembling here to do honor to your patron, to my mind, bespeaks the beginning of an era of intellectual progress, already too long delayed. I therefore heartily congratulate your Society on the advanced sentiment shown to encourage investigation into the lives of the many eminent men belonging to the Negro race, who are omitted in the histories by Caucasian authors and allowed to sleep the sleep of oblivion, by those who might rescue their memories and put on record the testimony of their deeds. It is not for me standing in this place, to criticize those who periodically appear before our Lyceums and discuss political topics. I do feel, however, that I am justified in urging that those who have the time and inclination should turn their attention to building up testimony to refute the charge of intellectual inferiority, which may easily be done, by putting in evidence the lives of our eminent men. For it is a truth, that allied by blood with the Negro race were some of the greatest men the world has produced. What follows is only a beginning of the flood of testimony furnished in almost every instance by Caucasian writers, which some day I hope to give to the world in extenso. Scientists and investigators in every line are crowding all the avenues of discovery, invention and literary research; they are surprising our credulity with the marvelous results of their investigations. Therefore, it is not amiss that something previously overlooked in regard to the colored man should come to light, and be marshalled as testimony in favor of his intellectual equality with the races of mankind, and further prove that he has always been equal to his opportunities. This investigation into the storehouse of literature particularly as it relates to colored authors, it will be seen, is a work of no little magnitude; it is both philosophical and profound. Something of its magnitude as a separate effort will appear from a consideration of the bibliographical fact, that it requires about thirty thousand volumes to contain even the names of the world's authors, and titles of their works, not estimating tracts, pamphlets or newspapers. Some one may inquire, "Why has not this in regard to the Colored race been brought forward before?" To this query Jefferson's answer to the Abbe Raynal in regard to Young America is quite appropriate.

When Raynal wondered why America has not produced celebrated men, Jefferson replied, "When we shall have existed as a nation as long as the Greeks before they produced a Homer, the Romans a Virgil, or the French a Racine, there will be room for astonishment." And what room would there be for astonishment if the people of Africa had not produced great men since the days when Sir John Hawkins commenced dealing in their living bodies, under authority of Queen Elizabeth. Would Lord Bacon have made himself the prince of philosophers if he had been brought to the Court of Elizabeth in chains from some tribe as savage as were his own ancestors at the time of the Roman invasion? If we were to find among the descendants of Africa, under all their present disadvantages, minds equal in genius and accomplishments to Bacon, Shakespeare, John Milton, or Sir Isaac Newton, might we not expect then, in a few hundred years, with equal advantages, to eclipse the glories of the Caucasian race? If literature is the measure of greatness, the answer, What has become of the literature of the ancient Britons, who were slaves at Rome in the time of Nero? We call upon the claimants of Caucasian superiority to bring it forward, and failing to do so, to abandon such an untenable claim.

In 1790, President Washington commenced the work of laying out the Federal City. For this work Major Peter Chas. L'Enfant was engaged. L'Enfant had been in the Army under Washington and was highly estimated. Associated with him was Mr. Andrew Ellicott, who engaged Banneker to assist. L'Enfant was an eccentric and highly tempered genius, very difficult to get along with. He was constantly in hot water with the President and Jefferson, particularly with the latter, whom it seems recommended him to Washington. Several times he threatened to abandon the work of laying out the city, and Washington was constantly in dread that he would carry his threat into execution and yielded every demand. At last L'Enfant made a demand that could not be accorded and upon being convinced of this, true to his previous threats, in a fit of high dudgeon gathered all his plans and papers and unceremoniously left. It seems, Daniel Carroll, who was one of the Commissioners, and the owner of the famous Mansion "Duddington," had built it outside L'Enfant lines and he against Washington's protest, tore it down. An interesting story is told of the Duddington House, North Carolina Avenue, Southeast. Daniel Carroll, the owner, who was one of the Commissioners to lay out the City, assumed against L'Enfant's protest, to build his house right in the center of what was intended for New Jersey Avenue. L'Enfant objected and explained the situation, but that not availing to stop the work he tore the house down. Washington was deeply offended at L'Enfant's act and ordered its restoration, but not, however, in the middle of New Jersey Avenue. The next largest proprietor was David Burns, a Scotchman, who owned the land south of the White House and including a part of the Mall. His daughter married Gen. John P. Van Ness, a member of Congress from New York, and at the death of her father became very rich. Van Ness was at one time Mayor of Washington and during his career lived in great style. He used to drive through the city in a fine carriage drawn by six white horses.

Through L'Enfant's unceremonious abandonment of his work, Washington was in despair, since it involved a defeat of all his cherished plans in regard to the "Federal City." This perturbation on his part was quickly ended, however, when it transpired that Banneker had daily for the purposes of calculation and practice, transcribed nearly all L'Enfant's field notes and through the assistance they afforded Mr. Andrew Ellicott, L'Enfant's assistant, Washington City was laid down very nearly on the original lines. It was while engaged in this work, 1791, that Banneker sent his Almanac to Jefferson.

L'Enfant took his plans as originally laid down for Washington, to Michigan and there sold them to Governor Woodward, and upon them the City of Detroit was laid out, Woodward Avenue corresponding to Pennsylvania Avenue in Washington. Those who are familiar with the plans of Detroit and Washington must have noticed the similarity which is quite remarkable. The original of both, however, being taken from Versailles, France, the Royal residence for many years of the Frency Kings. By this act the brain of the

Afro-American is indissolubly linked with the
Capital and nation. It is an indisputable evidence of the capacity of the colored man,
though as Banneker was mixed blood, his
grandmother being a white woman, his talents
may be, and probably will be ascribed to his
Caucasian reinforcement. He never married,
being rather disposed to solitude and the contemplation of his problems which required
absolute quiet, which quiet matrimony did not
offer.

In 1843 the Conference of the A. M. E.
Church, in session in Baltimore, appointed a
committee of three with Daniel A. Payne
(afterwards a Bishop in the connection) as
chairman, to report upon the possibility of finding the grave of Banneker and erecting a
monument over his remains. The Committee
went to Ellicott's Mills and made diligent in-
quiry as to the spot. Many old people in the
vicinity were consulted, but were only able to
describe the spot as near a certain tree, which
upon investigation was found to have disap-
peared, thus removing the only means of
identification. Dr. Payne was obliged to report that the Committee was unable to carry
out the order of the Conference to place a
monument over the grave of Benjamin
Banneker.

BANNEKER AND HIS TIMES

IN presenting Benjamin Banneker as proof of the intellectual capacity of the African and his descendants, we are not compelled to rest our case alone upon him, notwithstanding the fine showing that can be made with him.

The limits I have set myself, in marshalling the cases and testimony on the intellectual capacity of the African does not permit me to go outside the confines of the United States. Happily it is possible to find within its boundaries many intellectual giants that are entitled to rank with him. Immortals.

In this list I will name Thos. Fuller, the Mathematician; Booker T. Washington, Dr. James Derham, Briton and Jupiter Hammon, Alonzo Othello, Prince Hall, Capt. Paul Cuffee, John B. Russworm, Samuel E. Cornisly, Gen. Moses Horton, Bishop Rich. Allen, Rev. Absalom Jones, Phillis Wheatley, Dr. Peter Williams, Harry Hozier, Bishop Christopher Rush, John Stewart, Catherine Ferguson, Crispers Attuck, Daniel Coker, Elijah Johnson, Rt. Rev. James Varick, Father (Peter) Spencer, Peter Ogden, Rt. Rev. Francis Asbury, Stephen Hill, John Fortie, William J. Watkins, Mary Ann Hall, Rev. John Gloucester, John Chavis, Mrs. Jarena Lee, Salem Poor, Denmark Vesey, Emanuel Perira, Moses Roper, Samuel Frances, Louis Pachieco, Pompay Lamb, Hero of Story Point, July 15th, 1779; David Walker, Noah Caldwell Cannon, Robt. Benjamin Lewis, author of "Light and Truth," 1836.

BANNEKER

CHAPTER I

BENJAMIN BANNEKER, the Afric-American astronomer, was born in 1731 at Ellicott Mills, near Baltimore, Maryland, the son of Robert and Mary Banneker. The first that is known of the name of Banneker is that it was borne by an African prince, who, being captured and brought to America as a slave, was purchased by Molly Welsh, an English woman owning a small farm near the Patapsco river.

It was through the desire of his grandmother to have someone read to her from the Bible, that she taught her daughter's child to the extent of her own education, which joined to his natural powers, enabled him to become an expert mathematician. It was while working for George Ellicott, who erected the first mill in Baltimore county, that Banneker was induced to undertake the labor of calculating an almanac, which the Ellicotts had done some years ago and were going to discontinue. The immensity of the labor and mathematical knowledge required for the prosecution of such undertaking is in a measure brought to our comprehension by an examination of the history of the Gregorian calendar.

It is to be regretted that no portrait of Banneker has come down to us. Oil painting and engraving on copper was the only means known to that date for transmitting a portrait. It is true the silhouette method was used but it it was not satisfactory.

He is described by a gentleman who frequently met him at this time "as of a brown complexion, medium stature, of uncommonly soft, gentle manners, and of pleasing colloquial powers." Whatever others thought of him, the friendship of George Ellicott, the owner of the mills, himself a man of high literary attainments, never faltered. Ellicott's visits to Banneker were frequent. Finally he induced our timid star-gazer to venture such calculations as are set down in almanacs. But what was Ellicott's chagrin to find that his black friend's first prediction of an eclipse was false; an error had slipped into his calculations. Ellicott drew his attention to it. To his mingled surprise and delight, Banneker answered by letter, pointing out that he had been misled by a discrepancy between the two authors, Ferguson and Leadbeater. "Now, Mr. Ellicott," runs the letter, "two such learned gentlemen as the above-mentioned, one in direct opposition to the other, stagnate young beginners. But I hope that the stagnation will not be of long duration." In the same letter, speaking of the greatness of the task, he thus writes: "It is an easy matter for us, when a diagram is laid down before us, to draw one in resemblance to it; but it is a hard matter for a young tyro in astronomy, when only the elements for the prediction are laid down for him, to draw his diagram with any degree of certainty."

Of the labor of his work few of those can form an idea who would nowadays attempt such a task with all the assistance afforded by accurate tables and well-digested rules. Banneker had no aid whatever from men or tables; and Mr. George Ellicott, who promised him some astronomical tables and took them to him, declares that he had advanced unaided far in the preparation of the logarithms necessary for his purposes. A memorandum of his calculations points out other errors of Ferguson and of Leadbeater, both of whom, no doubt, would have been amazed had they been informed that their elaborate works had been reviewed and corrected by a negro in the then unheard-of-valley of the Patapsco.

The first almanac prepared by Banneker for publication was for the year 1792. The almanac-publishers of Baltimore gave a very flattering praise to the compiler.

Banneker himself was entirely conscious of the bearings of his case upon the position of his people; and, though remarkable for an habitual modesty, he solemnly claimed that his work had earned respect for the African race. In this spirit he wrote to Thomas Jefferson, then Secretary of State under Washington, transmitting a manuscript copy of his almanac. The letter—a fervent appeal for the down-trodden negro, and a protest against the injustice and inconsistency of his treatment by the people of the United States—is herewith given entire. I beg the reader as he peruses this letter to weigh its pleadings well, putting himself and our times in place of Jefferson and one hundred and twenty years ago.

Maryland, Baltimore County,
Near Ellicott's Lower Mills,

August 19th, 1791.

*To Thomas Jefferson, Secretary of State,
Philadelphia.*

SIR.—I am fully sensible of the greatness of
that freedom which I take on the present occasion; a liberty, which seemed to me scarcely
allowable, when I reflected on that distinguished and honorable station in which you
stand; and, the almost general prejudice and
prepossession which is prevalent in the world,
against those of my complexion.

I suppose it is a truth too well attested to
you to need a proof here, that we are a race of
beings who have long labored under the abuse
and censure of the world, and that we have
long been considered rather brutish, than as
human, and scarcely capable of mental endowments.

Sir, I hope I may safely admit, in conse-
quences of that report which hath reached me,
that you are a man far less inflexible in sentiments of this nature, than many others; that
you are measurably friendly, and ready to lend
your aid and assistance to our relief, from the
many distresses and numerous calamities to

which we are reduced. Now, Sir, if this is founded in truth, I apprehend you will embrace every opportunity to eradicate that train of absurd and false ideas and opinions, which so generally prevail with respect to us; and that your sentiments are concurrent with mine, which are—that one Universal Father hath given being to us all, and that He hath not only made us all of one flesh, but that He hath also, without partiality, afforded us all the same sensations, and endued us all with the same faculties; and that, however variable we may be in Society and Religion, however diversified in situation and color, we are all of the same family, and stand in the same relation to Him.

Sir, if these are sentiments of which you are fully persuaded, I hope you cannot but acknowledge that it is the indispensable duty of those who maintain for themselves the rights of human nature, and who profess the obligations of Christianity, to extend their power and influence to the relief of every part of the human race, from whatever burden or oppression they may unjustly labor under; and *this,* I apprehend, a full conviction of the truth, and obligations of these principles should lead all to.

Sir, I have long been convinced, that if your love for yourselves, and for those inestimable laws which preserve to you the rights of human nature. was founded on sincerity, you could not but be solicitous that every individual, of whatever rank or distinction, might with you equally enjoy the blessings thereof; neither could you rest satisfied, short of the most active diffusion of your exertions, in order to their promotion from any state of degration to which the unjustifiable cruelty and barbarism of men may have reduced them.

Sir, I freely and cheerfully acknowledge that I am of the African race; and, in that color which is natural to them, of the deepest dye; and it is under a sense of the most profound gratitude to the Supreme Ruler of the Universe, that I now confess to you that I am not under that state of tyrannical thraldom and inhuman captivity to which too many of my brethren are doomed; but that I have abundantly tasted of the fruition of those blessings, which proceed from that free and unequalled liberty with which you are favored, and which I hope you will willingly allow you have received from the immediate Hand of that Being from whom proceedeth "every good and perfect gift."

Sir, suffer me to recall to your mind that time in which the arms and tyranny of the British Crown were exerted with every powerful effort, in order to reduce you to a state of servitude. Look back, I entreat you, to the variety of dangers to which you were exposed; reflect on that time in which every human aid appeared unavailable, and in which even hope and fortitude wore the aspect of inability to the conflict; and you cannot but be led to a serious and grateful sense of your miraculous and providential preservation.

You cannot but acknowledge that the present freedom and tranquility which you enjoy you have mercifully received, and that it is the peculiar blessing of Heaven.

This, Sir, was a time in which you clearly saw into the injustice of a state of slavery, and in which you had just apprehensions of the horrors of its condition; it was now, Sir, that your abhorrence thereof was so excited that you publicly held forth this true and invaluable doctrine, which is worthy to be recorded and remembered in all succeeding ages, "We hold these truths to be self-evident, that all men are created equal, and that they are endowed by their Creator with certain inalienable rights, that amongst these are life, liberty, and the pursuit of happiness."

Here, Sir, was a time in which your tender feelings for yourselves engaged you thus to declare; you were then impressed with a proper idea of the just valuation of liberty, and the free possession of those blessings to which you were entitled by nature; but, Sir, how pitiable it is to reflect, that although you were so fully convinced of the benevolence of the Father of mankind, and of his equal and impartial distribution of those rights and privileges which He had conferred upon them, that you should, at the same time, counteract his mercies, in detaining, by fraud and violence, so numerous a part of my brethren, under groaning captivity and oppression; that you should, at the same time, be found guilty of that most criminal act, which you professedly detested in others, with respect to yourselves.

Sir, I suppose that your knowledge of the situation of my brethren is too extensive to need a recital here; neither shall I presume to prescribe methods by which they may be relieved, otherwise than by recommending to you, and to all others, to wean yourselves from those narrow prejudices which you have imbibed with respect to them, and, as Job proposed to his friends, "Put your souls in their souls' stead." Thus shall your hearts be en-larged with kindness and benevolence towards them, and thus shall you need neither the direction of myself nor others in what manner to proceed therein.

And now, Sir, although my sympathy and affection for my brethren hath caused my enlargement thus far, I ardently hope that your candor and generosity will plead with you in my behalf, when I make known to you that it was not originally my design, but that, having taken up my pen in order to direct to you, as a present, a copy of an Almanac which I have calculated for the ensuing year, I was unexpectedly and unavoidably led thereto.

This calculation, Sir, is the production of my arduous study, in this my advanced stage of life; for having long had unbounded desires to become acquainted with the secrets of nature, I have had to gratify my curiosity herein, through my own assiduous application to astronomical study, in which I need not recount to you the many difficulties and disadvantages I have had to encounter.

And, although I had almost declined to make my calculation for the ensuing year, in consequence of the time which I had allotted there-for being taken up at the Federal Territory, by the request of Mr. Andrew Ellicott; yet, finding myself under engagements to printers of this State, to whom I had communicated my design, on my return to my place of residence, I industriously applied myself thereto, which I hope I have accomplished with correctness and accuracy, a copy of which I have taken the liberty to direct to you, and which I humbly request you will favorably receive; and, although you may have the opportunity of perusing it after its publication, yet I chose to send it to you in manuscript previous thereto, that thereby you might not only have an earlier inspection, but that you might also view it in my own handwriting.

And now, Sir, I shall conclude, and subscribe myself with the most profound respect, Your most obedient, humble servant,

B. Banneker.

Mr. Thomas Jefferson,
Secretary of State, Philadelphia.

N. B.—Any communication to me may be had by a direction to Mr. Elias Ellicott, Baltimore Town.

Thomas Jefferson's reply to the above letter:

.. PHILADELPHIA, *August* 30th, 1791.

SIR.—I thank you sincerely for your letter of the 19th instant, and for the almanac it contained. Nobody wishes more than I do, to see such proofs as you exhibit that nature has given to our black brethren talents equal to the other colors of men, and that the appearance of a want of them is owing merely to the degraded condition of their existence, both in Africa and America. I can add, with truth, that nobody wishes more ardently to see a good system commenced for raising the condition, both of their body and mind, to what it ought to be, as fast as the imbecility of their present existence, and other circumstances which cannot be neglected, will admit.

I have taken the liberty of sending your almanac to Monsieur de Condorcet, Secretary of the Academy of Sciences at Paris, and a member of the Philanthropic Society, because I considered it as a document to which your whole color had a right, for their justification against the doubts which have been entertained of them.

I am with great esteem, Sir, your most obedient, humble servant,

THOMAS JEFFERSON.

MR. BENJAMIN BANNEKER,

Near Ellicott's Lower Mills, Baltimore Co.

CHAPTER II

THIS Molly Welsh, spoken of on a preceeding page, was a person of exceedingly fair complexion and moderate mental powers, had been an involuntary emigrant to America. When a servant on a cattle-farm in her native land, where milking formed a part of her duty, she was accused of stealing a bucket of milk, which a cow had kicked over. For this supposed offense, she was, by the stern laws of her country, sentenced to transportation, escaping a heavier penalty from the fact that she could read. On her arrival here she was, as was the custom, sold to defray the expenses of the voyage, for a term of seven years, and purchased by a tobacco planter on Patapsco river.

When her term of service had expired, land being of merely nominal value at that period, she was able to purchase the farm mentioned above. Here, needing assistance in her work, she bought in 1692 two negro men, one being the "Banneker" of whom we have spoken. The other slave proved an industrious and valuable servant, while Banneker seemed to show his royal blood by a decided disinclination for work.

After a few years their owner set them free. The diligent worker had meanwhile embraced the Christian religion; but the prince remained loyal to the faith of his ancestors, and retained his African name, being simply "Banneker." He was a man of bright intelligence and fine temper, with a very agreeable presence, dignified manners and contemplative habits.

Banneker died early, leaving his wife with four young children. The family tradition tells us nothing further of her until she had a daughter grown to womanhood. Mary, her oldest daughter, married early a native African. He had been purchased from a slave-ship by a planter living near her mother. His devotional turn of mind induced him early to become a member of the Church of England, and he received the name of Robert in baptism, upon which event his master gave him his freedom.

It was subsequent to his being a free man that he married Mary Banneker and assumed his wife's surname.

We learn, however, that seven years subsequent to the latter event he purchased a farm. This property was conveyed to him by deed, from Richard Gist, on the 10th of March, 1737. We thus learn indirectly that the parents of Benjamin Banneker were married about the year 1730. For this land Robert Banneker (recorded as Banneky) paid 7,000 pounds of tobacco, that article being used instead of money in the colony.

Immediately upon being possessed of this farm, which contained 100 acres, and was near that of his mother-in-law, Robert Banneker set about building a house, improving his land, and making a comfortable home for his family. Benjamin Banneker was six years old when his father made the above purchase. The date of his birth is recorded in his own handwriting in a quarto Bible, now in possession of one of his relatives. The earliest specimen of his handwriting begins with a note of the purchase of the Bible, thus:

"I bought this book of Honora Buchanan the 4th day of January, 1763. B. B."

"Benjamin Banneker was born November the 9th, in the year of the Lord God, 1731."

It is unfortunate that he did not complete his family record, but only added the death of his father.

"Robert Banneker departed this life July the 10th, 1759."

Few of the circumstances of the early life of the subject of our narrative are now known. According to the testimony of John Henden (a son of Banneker's oldest sister), his bright mind made him a great favorite with his grandmother, who found much pleasure in imparting to him all her small stock of knowledge in the department of letters. She much desired he should grow up a religious man, in furtherance of which view it was her delight to have him read to her from a large Bible which she had imported from England. After he had learned to read he attended a small school, where a few white and two or three colored children received together instruction from the same master.

CHAPTER III

IT was in this school that his love of study first became apparent. Jacob Hall, who was a fellow-pupil with Banneker, and was intimately acquainted with him during his whole life, said that, as a boy, he was never fond of play or any light amusement; that "all his delight was to dive into his books."

Benjamin Banneker's opportunities for study under a teacher were very limited, and of short duration. The school was only open during the winter season, and he ceased to attend it after he had grown large enough to assist his father in his labors of the farm; but, happily, his love of reading and desire to acquire knowledge remained with him.

After his youth was passed, he still continued to reside with his parents, and at the time of his father's death, which, we have seen, took place in 1759, he was twenty-eight years old.

Robert Banneker left to his widow and to his son, as joint heirs, the dwelling in which they lived and seventy-two acres of land. The remaining twenty-eight acres he divided between his three daughters.

Despite the studious habits of Benjamin Banneker, he was a good farmer, and very industrious in his work. He had a fine garden and well selected assortment of fruit trees. He kept two horses and several cows, and was very skillful in the management of his bees. All his work kept him closely engaged, except during the winter, leaving but scant time for his favorite studies, but from the fact that life was for him a school, and whether he was following the plow or reaping his grain, his contemplative mind found time for development.

In order to picture to ourselves the difficult circumstances through which Banneker's genius struggled, we must recall the wildness of the country, and the merely dawning civilization of the period. Although there were, in this section of the country, many settlers, there were still vast tracts of primeval forest, where the native animals found ample range.

Here would be found deer, wild turkeys, and other timid creatures, while close at hand lurked their destroyers, the wolf, the panther, and the wild-cat, whose nightly cries disturbed the neighboring settlers. These animals had full possession of the valley where Ellicott City centers until the year 1772, at which period Banneker was forty-one years old.

When he was twenty-one years old there were only two sea-going vessels owned in Baltimore, and he was forty-two years old before any newspaper was published there. "The Maryland Gazette and Commercial Advertiser" issued its first number August 20th, 1773. Previous to this, "Green's Maryland Gazette," first issued in 1745, at Annapolis, was the sole advertising medium of the Province.

The one or two public stores to be found at that time in Baltimore, Joppa, and Annapolis, were so far out of reach of the planters of Elk Ridge, that they were accustomed to make their own importations. The size and luxury of these fluctuated with the London tobacco market. When this commodity commanded a good price, they indulged in large importations, purchasing much more than they needed for their own use. Each of these importing planters had a store-house, which received the varied result of the importation.

After selecting all that was required for home use, the surplus was disposed of to non-importing planters and small farmers.

It was the custom on large plantations to fire a cannon at sunrise, to summon all hands

to the business of the day; but when this cannon was fired at sunset, it was a notification
that a supply of goods had arrived, which
would be offered for sale or barter the next and
following days.

It was on such stores as this that Banneker
was compelled to depend during the earlier
period of his life.

Every description of farming implement,
from a plow to a rake, was purchased here;
manufacturers being discouraged by the home
government. Even shoes were thus procured.
Rich and poor all met here to purchase, many
hurrying to get a first choice of the products
of the looms of Great Britain and India. Here
could be had brocades, embroideries, china,
glassware, and mirrors, engravings, choice
editions of classical writers, wines, and
groceries.

Goods were sold at these private stores that
would make a modern country store proprietor
stand aghast at the thought of purchasing.
Specimens of these early importations, still
carefully preserved in some old families, do
not suffer by comparison with the production
of modern times.

When Banneker, as well as his neighbors,
visited these private store-houses, designing to

purchase any bulky commodities, they would be accompanied by one or more pack-horses, according to the proposed extent of their purchases. There were no roads over which even a wagon could travel, except that from Frederick to Baltimore, with a branch road to Annapolis. Carriages were a thing unseen and almost unheard of. There was a net-work of "bridle-roads," as they were termed; mere winding paths, connecting parts of the country together. From Frederick, such a road was used to communicate with Georgia.

"Rolling roads" were those over which tobacco was taken to its place of shipment. Their name suggests the manner in which the tobacco was propelled. After being packed in hogsheads and securely hooped, each hogshead was consigned to the care of two men, who rolled it over and over to the place of shipment. Elk Ridge Landing, on the Patapsco River, near the residents of "Elk Ridge," as that large section of country was called. Shipments to London, and importations, were generally through the port of Joppa, the tobacco sent from Elk Ridge Landing being reshipped at the latter place.

Joppa took precedence of Baltimore in commercial importance until the year 1773. It was the seat of the courts of Baltimore County, in which at that time Harford County was included. At the above date the county was divided, and the northern part named after the proprietary of the time. This change was fatal to the town of Joppa. On this spot, where there was a court house, four-story warehouses and many dwellings built of imported brick, there now remains but one dwelling. This is the property of Mr. James Murray, a large landed proprietor. When the tide of prosperity receded, Joppa was stranded, and from that time the buildings served as a quarry or brickyard, from which the neighboring farmers purchased material for building. Bricks were bought there as late as 1849, when the supply came to an end.

The only local evidence that this town ever existed is found in the graveyard, where we may read on marble brought from London:

IN MEMORY OF
DAVID McCULLOH,
MERCHANT IN JOPPA,
WHO DIED THE 7TH DAY OF SEPT., 1766,
AGED 48 YEARS.

The former site of Joppa may be seen to the left, in traveling northward over the Gunpowder bridge, on the Philadelphia, Wilmington and Baltimore Railroad.

During this simple state of society, people learned much self-reliance. Until Banneker was forty-two years old, there were no workshops except of a private character, not even a blacksmith's shop. Each plantation and family had its own shop or shops. There, horses were shod with imported shoes, and farming implements mended; all sorts of repairs were made in these shops. The blacksmith, the cobbler, the tinker, the tailor, were all traveling artisans. Plying their trade in a considerable area of country, they became necessarily depositories of local news, for which they were none the less welcome, as they made their various trips.

We shall see presently how desirable it would have been for the young Banneker to have had some delicate tools fashioned to assist him in an intricate piece of mechanism; and it is hard to realize how he was able to attain so high a degree of scientific culture and skilled manipulation, as he manifested at this time, when he was seemingly without opportunity for study or observation, and even without tools to aid him. His genius, however, developed in combatting difficulties.

During his earlier manhood he found a great delight in mechanics, but had passed the meridian of life before astronomy became *the one* study to which all others yielded precedence.

When he had seen no timepieces but a sundial and a watch, he made himself a clock which struck the hours, and was an admirable time-keeper. The works were of hard wood, cut out with a knife. In 1773, this clock had been running twenty years, and was naturally regarded as a great curiosity. When the clock was completed, Banneker was twenty-two years old. The fame of this achievement spread far and wide, and caused people to marvel much over this self-taught son of Africa, who was thus outstripping his neighbors of Anglo-Saxon parentage.

CHAPTER IV

IN 1772, when Banneker was forty-one years old, a new field opened to his mental vision. It was the advent of the Ellicott family, who at this time moved from Pennsylvania and settled in Banneker's neighborhood. These were men of great force and foresight. Arriving by water at Elk Ridge Landing, they took their wagons apart, and carried them, a piece at a time, into the wilderness, where they proposed to erect flour mills. Here they cleared away the forest and built dams, and began to build mills (with a view to exporting flour) in a country where no grain was raised except for family use.

Their neighbors were not slow to visit this scene of action, most of them protesting against the folly of the work, as there never was any grain for sale in the neighborhood, the main product of the soil being tobacco.

These Ellicotts had examined the character of the country before deciding to settle there. They considered it peculiarly adapted to the growth of cereals, and they told their neighbors that "a demand would create a supply," and that there would be wheat to grind as soon as there was a mill to grind it. Meantime, they had set an example of what could be done, by planting crops upon their own land at the same time that their building operations were going on.

By the time that their first mill was ready to run, there was no lack of grain being offered for sale, but the first flour was made from the growth of their fields. In a few years, the agricultural system of the community was revolutionized, and the district became noted for its abundant crops of grain.

The fame of Banneker's clock had been the cause of an early acquaintance between him and his miller neighbors. They found him and his mother living together in great comfort and plenty. The boarding-houses for the workmen who erected the mills, and other buildings for Ellicott & Co., were largely supplied with provisions from the farm of Banneker. His mother, Mary Banneker, attended to the marketing, bringing for sale poultry, vegetables, fruit, and honey.

The mother of Banneker was (her opportunities considered) a woman of uncommon intelligence. She had a knowledge of the properties and uses of herbs, which was often of advantage to her neighbors. Her appearance was imposing, her complexion a pale copper color, similar to that of the fairest Indian tribes, and she had an ample growth of long black hair, which never became gray. Her grandsons, the children of one of her daughters, used to speak with admiration of her many good qualities and her remarkable activity. They loved to relate that when she wished to prepare a basket of chickens for market, "she would run them down and catch them without assistance." This continued her practice when she was over seventy years of age.

The erection of the milling machinery was watched with great interest by Banneker, and he continued to make frequent visits to the mills after their operations had ceased to be a novelty.

A store had naturally grown up beside the mills, in an apartment of which, very soon, a post-office was opened and a daily mail established. This store became a place of resort for the planters and others, to whom it served as an exchange, where, after selling or buying and receiving their mail, they tarried to discuss the news of the day.

The conversational powers of Banneker being of the first order, he was encouraged by the proprietors to make them frequent visits, and he was thus introduced to many strangers.

When he could be induced to lay aside the modest reserve for which he was conspicuous, all were pleased to listen to him. His mind was filled with volumes of traditionary lore, from which he would relate various anecdotes of the first occupation of the country by the emigrants; their disappointments and difficulties, and final successes; when, ceasing their fruitless search for gold, they settled down to the cultivation of the soil.

Occasionally, Banneker would allude to his own life, and his laborious pursuit of knowledge, unaided by the auxiliaries he then enjoyed through the kindness of the owners of the mills.

There was an especial sympathy between one of the younger members of the Ellicott family and Banneker. This was George Ellicott, the father of Martha Tyson.

He had been a mere youth when the family settled at Ellicott's Mills. That he had much energy and business capacity, we may know from the fact that the present road from Frederick to Baltimore was surveyed and laid out by him when he was seventeen years old. It is three miles shorter than the previous road. George Ellicott had a great love for the science of astronomy, in which he was well versed. Conceiving early a high estimate of Banneker's powers, he found pleasure in making him frequent visits, and furnishing him with such books and instruments as would aid him in his studies.

CHAPTER V

WE find from the records of the Columbia Historical Society, Volume 20, 1917, as follows:

Benj. Banneker is known to the residents of the District of Columbia as connected with Ellicott in surveying the ten miles square. Little is known of his efforts in literature, astronomy and mathematics.

The following notes of Banneker are found first published in his Almanac, 1792, and republished with abridgement in 1793, from which we are making extracts.

It was written by Banneker's esteemed friend and admirer, James McHenry, who was afterward senator from the state of Maryland, and evidently a man who appreciated intellect, whether in the soul of the black or white, that at the time Banneker wrote his *Plea of Peace* in 1793, there existed wars between the United States and American Indians, between the British nation and Tuppar Saib, between the planters of St. Domingo and their African slaves, and also between the French nation and

Germany. Banneker's *Plea of Peace* ends with
the following lines: "The son of man came
into the world not to destroy men's lives, but
to save them."

The Georgetown weekly Ledger of March
12, 1791, speaks of the arrival at Georgetown
of Ellicott and L'Enfant, who were attended
by one Benj. Banneker, an Ethiopean, whose
abilities as a surveyor and astronomer would
be used in laying out the city of Washington.
That his color did not affect his reputation is
proven by the friendship of Washington, Jefferson and Ellicott and many distinguished
scientists in Europe, who called him the "Afric-
American Astronomer."

All who had known his grandfather, the
African prince, conceded that it was from *him*
that the student grandson inherited the fine
qualities of mind through which the name of
Banneker became famous. His superiority
over other men of his race made him an object
of interest with all who knew him. They ac-
cepted his advancement in knowledge as a
harbinger of better days for his people. His
cottage came to be much frequented by
strangers, as well as by the neighboring gentry.
It was in this retired abode that Elizabeth Ellicott made him a visit in company with some of

her friends in 1790. His door stood wide open, and so closely was his mind engaged that they entered without being seen. Immediately upon observing them he arose, and with much courtesy invited them to be seated. The large oval table at which Banneker sat was strewn with works on astronomy and with scientific appurtenances. He alluded to his love of the study of astronomy and mathematics as quite unsuited to a man of his class, and regretted his slow advancement in them, owing to the laborious nature of his agricultural engagements, which obliged him to spend the greater portion of his time in the fields.

Whilst they were engaged in conversation his clock struck the hour, and at their request he gave them an account of its construction. With his inferior tools, with no other model than a borrowed watch, it had cost him long and patient labor to perfect it. It required much study to produce a concert of correct action between the hour, minute, and second machinery, and to cause it to strike the hours. He acknowledged himself amply repaid for all his cares in its construction by the precision with which it marked the passing time. His mother had died previously to this, and he was the sole occupant of his dwelling There had been a very strong affection between this mother and her gifted son.

Banneker was very assiduous in all his pursuits, and had much interest in agriculture, but finding his material occupations interfere so much with his design of devoting himself more closely to science, he sought out some plan by which he might obtain the coveted leisure, and hesitated long before deciding on an arrangement adapted to his condition. He finally determined to convey his land to Ellicott & Co., reserving to himself a life-estate in it. By this plan he received an annuity of £12 a year. Estimating this yearly payment by the probable duration of his life, he remarked to his assignees, "I believe I shall live fifteen years, and consider my land worth £180, Maryland currency. By receiving £12 a year for fifteen years, I shall, in the contemplated time, receive its full value; if, on the contrary, I die before that day, you will be at liberty to take possession." On making this change in his affairs, he deemed some explanation necessary as an apology for his apparent selfishness.

He referred to his desire to increase his knowledge on subjects to which his attention had been directed from his youth, and to his inability from physical infirmities, to perform

much laborious exercise; his land would thus
be poorly cultivated, and poverty, an evil he
much dreaded, increase upon him. Should he
attempt to divide his small property, by will,
among his nearest relatives, the parcels would
be too small to be of service to any. If he gave
it all to two or three, they would become ob-
jects of envy. Under the pressure of these
conflicting views, he avowed that he felt ex-
cusable for making an arrangement exclusively
for his own benefit.

Being now relieved from the necessity for
constant toil, he revelled as never before in his
astronomical studies. Banneker never married,
nor can we learn that his mind was ever turned
to the thought of such a possibility as marriage.
He was possessed of a rare self-reliance. His
"unbounded desires to become acquainted with
the secrets of nature" caused him to need little
society. His sisters, Minta Black and Molly
Morton, lived near him, and cared for his
necessities.

Having ceased a life of labor, he mostly
passed the night, wrapped in his cloak and lying
prostrate on the ground, in contemplation of
the heavenly bodies.

At dawn he retired to rest, and spent a part
of the day in repose, but does not seem to have

required as much sleep as ordinary mortals. Still cultivating sufficient ground to give him needful exercise, he might often be seen hoeing his corn, cultivating his garden, or trimming his fruit trees. Sometimes he would be found watching the habits of his bees.

Occasionally, as a relaxation from his favorite studies, he would pass the twilight hour seated beneath a large chestnut tree, which grew on the hillside near his house, playing on the flute or violin. He loved music, and had some little skill in using either of these instruments.

*   *   *   *   *   *

One matter, personal to himself, gave him great pleasure in the retrospect that during his stay in Washington, *he had not tasted either wine or spirituous liquors.*

He had experienced the fact that it was unwise for him to indulge, ever so slightly, in stimulating drinks. On this occasion he said, "I feared to trust myself even with wine, lest it steal away the little sense I have." He was a noble example of what may be accomplished by a firm resolve.

Before entering upon his engagements with Major Ellicott, he had surmounted the difficulties alluded to in his letter to George Ellicott, of October, 1789. On his returning from his journey, he completed his first almanac, and arranged for its publication in the year 1792.

We subjoin, without abridgement, the very comprehensive title-page of the Afric-American astronomer's first almanac:

BENJAMIN BANNEKER'S
PENNSYLVANIA, DELAWARE, MARYLAND, AND VIRGINIA
ALMANAC
AND
EPHEMRIS
FOR THE YEAR OF OUR LORD,
1792.

Being Bissestile or Leap Year, and the sixteenth year of American Independence, which commenced July 4th, 1776. Containing the motions of the Sun and Moon, the true places and aspects of the Planets, the Rising and Setting of the Sun, and the Moon, etc., the Lunations, Conjunctions, Eclipses, Judgments of the Weather, Festivals, and other remarkable days. Days for holding the Supreme and Circuit courts of the United States, as also the usual courts in Pennsylvania, Delaware, Maryland, and Virginia; also several useful Tables and valuable Recipes; various selections from the common-place Book of the Kentucky Philosopher, an American sage; with interesting and entertaining Essays in Prose and Verse, the whole comprising a greater, more pleasing and useful variety than any work of the kind and price in North America.

We also give the printer's advertisement.

Baltimore; Printed and sold Wholesale and Retail by William Goddard and James Angell, at their Printing-office in Market Street; sold also by Mr. Joseph Cruikshank, Printer in Market Street, and Mr. Daniel Humphreys, Printer in South Front Street, Philadelphia, and by Messrs. Hanson and Bond, Printers, Alexandria, Va.

Annexed to the title-page was a card from William Goddard and James Angell, from which we extract the following:

"The editors of the Pennsylvania, Delaware, Maryland, and Virginia Almanac feel themselves gratified in the opportunity of presenting to the public, through the medium of their press, what must be considered an extraordinary effort of genius—a complete and accurate Ephemeris for the year 1792, calculated by a sable descendant of Africa, who, by this specimen of ingenuity, evinces to demonstration that

mental powers and endowments are not the ex-
clusive excellence of white people; but that the
rays of science may alike illumine the minds of
men of every clime, however they may differ
in the color of their skin, particularly those
whom tyrant custom hath taught us to depreci-
ate as a race inferior in intellectual.capacity.

"They flatter themselves that a philanthropic
public, in this enlightened era, will be induced
to give their patronage and support to this
work, not only on account of its intrinsic merit
(it having met the approbation of several of
the most distinguished astronomers in America,
particularly the celebrated Mr. Rittenhouse),
but from similar motive to those which induced
the editors to give this calculation the preference—the desire of drawing modest merit from
obscurity, and controverting the long established, illiberal prejudice against them.

"The editors of Banneker's Almanac have
taken the liberty of annexing a letter from Mr.
James McHenry, containing particulars respecting Benjamin, which it is presumed will
prove more acceptable to the reader than anything further in the prefactory way.

BALTIMORE, *August 20th, 1791.*

MESSRS. GODDARD AND ANGELL.

Benjamin Banneker, a free negro, has calculated an almanac for the ensuing year, 1792, which, being desirous to dispose of to the best advantage, he has requested me to aid his application to you for that purpose. Having fully satisfied myself with respect to his title to this kind of authorship, if you can agree with him for the price of his work, I may venture to assure you, it will do you credit as editors, while it will afford you the opportunity to encourage talents that have thus far surmounted the most discouraging circumstances and prejudices.

This man is about fifty-eight years of age. He was born in Baltimore Co.

His father and mother were enabled to send him to an obscure school, where he learned, when a boy, reading, writing, and arthmetic as far as double fractions, and to leave him at their deaths a few acres of land, upon which he has supported himself ever since by means of economy and constant labor, and preserved a fair reputation.

To struggle incessantly against want is no way favorable to improvement. What he learned, however, he did not forget; for as

some hours of leisure will occur in the most
toilsome life, he availed himself of them—not
to read and acquire knowledge from writings
of genius and discovery, for of such he had
none, but to digest and apply, as occasion presented, the few principles of the few rules of
arithmetic which he had been taught at school.

This kind of mental exercise formed his
chief amusement, and soon gave him a facility
in calculation that was often serviceable to his
neighbors, and at length attracted the attention of the Messrs. Ellicott, a family remarkable for their ingenuity and turn for the use
of mechanics.

It is about three years since Mr. George Ellicott lent him "Mayer's Tables," "Ferguson's
Astronomy," "Leadbeater's Lunar Tables,"
and some astronomic instruments.   .   .   .

These books and instruments, the first of the
kind he had ever seen, opened a new world to
Benjamin, and from thenceforward he em-
ployed his leisure in astronomical researches.
He now took up the idea of the calculations for
an almanac, and actually completed an entire
set for the last year, upon his original stock of
arithmetic.

Encouraged by his first attempt, he entered
upon his calculations for 1792, which he began

and finished without the least information or
assistance from any person or other books than
those I have mentioned, so that whatever merit
is attached to his present performance, it is
peculiarly and exclusively his own.

I have been the more careful to investigate
those particulars and to ascertain their reality,
as they form an interesting fact in the history
of man; and, as you may want them to gratify
curiosity, I have no objection to your selecting
them for your account of Benjamin.

I consider this negro as a fresh proof that
the powers of the mind are disconnected with
the color of the skin, or, in other words, a
striking contradiction to Mr. Hume's doctrine,
that "the negroes are naturally inferior to the
whites, and unsusceptible of attainments in arts
and sciences." In every civilized country, we
shall find thousands of whites liberally edu-
cated, and who have enjoyed greater opportunities for instruction than this negro, his in-
feriors in those intellectual acquirements and
capacities that form the most characteristic
features in the human race.

But the system that would assign to those degraded blacks an origin different from the
whites, if it is not ready to be deserted by
philosophers, must be relinquished as similar

instances multiply; and that such must frequently happen, cannot well be doubted, *should no check impede the progress of humanity,* which, meliorating the condition of slavery necessarily leads to its final extinction. Let, however, the issue be what it will, I cannot but wish on this occasion to see the public patronage keep pace with my black friend's merit.

I am, gentlemen, your most obedient servant,

JAMES McHENRY.

James McHenry was one of the most prominent men of Baltimore, and was several times honored by his fellow-citizens with positions of trust and dignity. He was elected a Senator of Maryland in 1781, but resigned his seat in 1786. He was also one of the commissioners for framing the Constitution of the United States, and with his colleagues signed that instrument in 1787.

On the election of John Adams to the Presidency of the United States, in 1797, James McHenry, as Secretary of War, became a member of his cabinet.

CHAPTER VI

BANNEKER was an adept in the solution of difficult mathematical problems. They were in his day, much more than at present, the pastime of persons of culture.

Such questions were frequently sent to him by scholars in different parts of the country, who wished to test his capacity. He never failed to return a solution, sometimes accompanying it by questions in rhyme of his own composition.

Charles W. Dorsey, a planter of Elk Ridge, at one time a clerk in the store of Ellicott & Co., very kindly furnished the author, in November, 1852, with the following recollections of Banneker, and also with one of those rhymed questions to which we have alluded:

"In the year 1800 I commenced my engagements in the store at Ellicott's Mills, where my first acquainance with Benjamin Banneker began. He often came to the store to purchase articles for his own use, and, after hearing him converse, I was always anxious to wait upon him. After making his purchases, he usually

went to the part of the store where George
Ellicott was in the habit of sitting, to converse
with him about the affairs of our government,
and other matters. He was very precise in
conversation and exhibited deep reflection.
His deportment, whenever I saw him, was perfectly upright and correct, and he seemed to
be acquainted with everything of importance
that was passing in the country.

"I recollect to have seen his almanacs in my
father's house, and believe they were the only
ones used in the neighborhood at the time. He
was a large man and inclined to be fleshy. He
was far advanced in years when I first saw him.

"I remember being once at his house, but do
not recollect anything of the comforts of the
establishment, nor of the old clock, about which
you queried.

"He was fond of, and well qualified to
work out, abstruse questions in arithmetic. I
remember he brought to the store one which
he had composed himself and presented to
George Ellicott for solution. I had a copy,
which I have since lost, but the character and
deportment of the man were so wholly different
from anything I had ever seen in one of his
color; his question made so deep an impres-
sion on my mind that I have ever since retained

a perfect recollection of it, except two lines, which do not alter the sense.

"I remember George Ellicott was engaged in making out the answer, and cannot now say how he succeeded, but have no doubt he did. I have thus briefly given you my recollections of Benjamin Banneker. I was young when he died, and doubtless many incidents, from the time which has since elapsed, have passed from my recollection."

The following is the question:

A cooper and vintner sat down for a talk,
Both being so groggy that neither could walk;
Says cooper to vintner, "I'm the first of my trade,
There's no kind of vessel but what I have made,
And of any shape, sir, just what you will,
And of any size, sir, from a tun to a gill."
"Then," says the vintner, "you're the man for me.
Make me a vessel, if we can agree.
The top and the bottom diameter define,
To bear that proportion as fifteen to nine,
Thirty-five inches are just what I crave,
No more and no less in the depth will I have;
Just thirty-nine gallons this vessel must hold,
Then I will reward you with silver or gold,—
Give me your promise, my honest old friend."
"I'll make it tomorrow, that you may depend!"
So, the next day, the cooper, his work to discharge,
Soon made the new vessel, but made it too large;
He took out some staves, which made it too small,
And then cursed the vessel, the vintner, and all.
He beat on his breast, "By the powers" he swore
He never would work at his trade any more.
Now, my worthy friend, find out if you can,
The vessel's dimensions, and comfort the man!

BENJAMIN BANNEKER.

Benj. Hallowell, of Alexandria, solved this problem: the greater diameter of Banneker's tub must be 24.745 inches; the less diameter, 14.8476.—See Maryland Historical Society Publication.

Banneker continued the publication of almanacs for ten years, after which declining health caused him to discontinue his calculations.

His time, during this later period of his life, was much taken up with the visitors whom his fame had attracted to his simple home.

Of all who visited him, we find in only one published work any account of an interview with this extraordinary man.

We extract from this work, long since out of print, *Memoir of Susannah Mason, by her daughter, R. Mason.*

"We found the venerable star-gazer under a wide-spreading pear tree laden with delicious fruit. He came forward to meet us, and bade us welcome to his lowly dwelling. It was built of logs, one story in height, and was surrounded by an orchard. In one corner of the room was a clock of his own construction, which was a true herald of departing hours. He took down from a shelf a little book, wherein he registered the names of those by whose

visits he felt particularly honored, and recorded
my mother's name upon the list. He then
diffidently, but very respectfully, requested her
acceptance of one of his almanacs in manuscript."

In the course of a few days, this lady sent
Banneker a rhymed letter, which afterwards
circulated through the newspapers of the day.
We copy it from the same work from whence
the preceding was taken.

"An address to Benjamin Banneker, the
African astronomer, who presented the author
with a manuscript almanac in 1796.

"Transmitted on the wings of fame,
Thine *eclat* sounding with thy name,
Well pleased I heard, 'ere 'twas my lot,
To see thee in thy humble cot,
That Genius smiled upon thy birth,
And application called it forth;
That times and tides thou couldst presage,
And traverse the celestial stage,
Where shining orbs their circles run,
In swift rotation round the sun.

* * * * * *

Some men, who private walks pursue,
Whom fame ne'er ushered into view,
May run their race, and few observe
To right or left, if they should swerve;
Their blemishes would not appear
Beyond their lines a single year.
But thou, a man exalted high,
Conspicuous in the world's keen eye,
On record now thy name's enrolled;
And future ages will be told

There lived a man named BANNEKER
An Africa Astronomer !
Thou need'st to have a special care,
Thy conduct with thy talent square,
That no contaminating vice
Obscure thy lustre in our eyes."

Some time after receiving this communication, he sent to its author the following letter, which we copy literally:

August 26th, 1797.

DEAR FEMALE FRIEND.—I have thought of you every day since I saw you last, and of my promise in respect of composing some verses for your amusement, but I am very much indisposed, and have been, ever since that time. I have a constant pain in my head, a palpitation in my flesh, and, I may say, I am attended with a complication of disorders, at this present writing, so that I cannot with any pleasure or delight gratify your curiosity in that particular at this present time, yet I may say, my will is good to oblige you, if I had it in my power; because you gave me good advice, and edifying language, in that piece of poetry which you was pleased to present unto me; and I can but love and thank you for the same; and, if it should ever be in my power to be serviceable to you in

any measure, your reasonable request shall be
armed with the obedience of
Your sincere friend and well wisher,

BENJAMIN BANNEKER.

MRS. SUSANNAH MASON.

N. B.—The above is mean writing done with
trembling hands.

This letter was directed to the care of Cas-
sandra Ellicott, afterwards married to Joseph
Thornburg, of the mercantile house of Thornburg, Miller & Webster, Baltimore.

We give some of the old astronomer's notes,
which are found in close proximity to his calculations of eclipses and other scientific work.
We learn from some of these observations how
fully he was alive to all that was beautiful or
remarkable about him.

"Our distilled spirits are like unto the water
of the river of Phrygia, which, if drank spar-
ingly, purges the brains and cures madness, but
otherwise it infects the brains and creates
madness."

"2 Kings, chapter 23d, verse 11, 'And he
took away the horses that the kings of Judah
had given to the sun.' "

"August 27th, 1797. Standing by my door,

I heard the discharge of a gun, and in four or five seconds of time the small shot came rattling about me, one or two of which struck the house, which plainly demonstrates that the velocity of sound is greater than that of a cannon-bullet. B. Banneker."

"22nd of Dec., 1790. About 3 o'clock A. M., I heard a sound, and felt the shock, like unto heavy thunder. I went out, but could not observe any cloud above the horizon. I therefore concluded it must be a great earthquake in some quarter of the globe."

"1803, Feb. 3d. In the morning part of the day there arose a very dark cloud, followed by snow and hail, a flash of lightning and a loud thunder-crash, and then the storm abated until afternoon, when another cloud arose at the same point, viz., the northwest, with a beautiful shower of snow. But what beautified the snow was the brightness of the sun, which was near setting at the time."

He wrote the following account of the locust years of his time in 1800:

"The first great locust year that I remember was in 1749. I was then about seventeen years old, when thousands of them came and were creeping about the bushes. I then imagined they came to eat and destroy the fruit of the

earth, and would occasion a famine in the land.
I therefore began to kill and destroy them, but
soon saw that the labor was in vain, and therefore gave over my pretension. Again, in the
year 1766, which is seventeen years after their
first appearance to me, they made a second,
and appeared to me as numerous as the first.
I then being about thirty-four years of age had
more sense than to endeavor to destroy them,
knowing they were not so pernicious to the
fruits of the earth as I did imagine they would
be.

"Again in the year 1783, which was seventeen years from their second appearance to me,
they made their third, and may be expected
again in 1800, which is seventeen years since
their third appearance to me. So that I may
venture to express it, their periodical return is
seventeen years; but they, like the comets,
make a short stay with us.

"I like to forget to inform, that if their lives
are short, they are merry. They begin to sing
or make a noise from the first they come out
of the earth till they die."

On the subject of his bees, he writes as
follows:

"In the month of January, 1797, on a pleas-
ant day for the season, I observed my honey

bees, and they seemed to be very busy, all but one hive. Upon examination, I found all the bees had evacuated this hive, and left not a drop of honey behind them. On the 9th of February ensuing, I killed the neighboring hive of bees on a special occasion, and found a great quantity of honey, considering the season, which, I imagine, the stronger had violently taken from the weaker, and the weaker had pursued them to their home, resolved to be benefited by their labor or die in the contest."

The commonplace book of the old astronomer gives ample assurance that his love for science had not diminished his prudent regard for the common affairs of life.

We give some of his memoranda:

"Sold on the 2d of April, 1795, to Butler, Edwards, and Kiddy, the right of an Almanac for the year 1796, for the sum of eighty dollars, equal to £30."

"On the 30th of April, 1795, lent John Ford five dollars—£1 17s. 6d."

"12th of December, 1797, bought a pound of candles, at 1s. 8d."

"Sold to John Collins two quarts dried peaches, 6d., one quart mead, 4d."

"On the 26th of March came Joshua Sanks

with three or four bushels of turnips to feed the cows."

"On the 13th of April, 1803, planted peas and sowed cabbage seed."

These domestic mementos occupy a strange proximity with entries of a more dignified nature, being occasionally found on the same page with a notice of astronomical character.

Benjamin Banneker possessed a remarkably mild and philosophic temperament, which was often manifested by his forbearance to his ignorant neighbors, who trespassed on his private rights, and to the boys of his vicinity who were in the constant habit of robbing his orchard. All his fruit was of the best kind, and his cherries and pears were in high favor with the youthful population, which had grown to be quite a formidable body in the last years of his life.

They would call respectfully at his door, ask and obtain permission to partake of some of his fruit, and afterwards retire; then, when he was shut up in his house immersed in calculations, they would return and strip his trees; thus he was often deprived of his fruit, and sometimes even before it had reached maturity.

For this he has been heard to remonstrate with the young culprits, and offer them an allowance of one-half, if they would leave him in undisturbed possession of the other half; but all to no purpose.

To a friend who once visited him in summer, he expressed his regret that he had no fruit to present him worthy of acceptance, adding, "I have no influence with the rising generation; all my arguments have failed to induce them to set bounds to their wants." He was not, however, left without a hope from the powerful influence of good examples sometimes at hand.

On this subject he remarked at the same time, "It has been said, 'Evil communications corrupt good manners;' I hope to live to hear that 'Good communications correct bad manners,'" a sentiment we find noted down amongst his manuscripts.

The situation of the astronomer's dwelling was one which would be admired by every lover of nature. Aside from furnishing a fine field for the observation of celestial phenomena, it commanded a prospect of the near and distant hills of the Patapsco river, which have always been celebrated for their picturesque beauty. A never-failing spring gushed forth beneath a large golden willow tree in the midst of his orchard.

The health of Banneker, as he approached
the evening of his days, often suffered from
complaints produced by his long patient astronomical observations, continued throughout all
seasons of the year.

His last recorded observations were for the
month of January, 1804, and are contained in
his commonplace book. After that period his
writing appears but once, when we find the
name "Benjamin Banneker," with the date
"1805," written by a trembling hand, on a torn
and stitched leaf of his volume of manuscript
almanacs. This is his last known penmanship.

*   *   *   *   *   *

CHAPTER VII

HOWEVER unfavorable the circumstances over which Banneker's genius triumphed, he was not without advantages. He was born *free,* the son of a *free man.* His father, and his grandfather before him, had experienced for only a short period the mental influences of a state of dependence. Banneker understood and respected his privileges, not the least among which was the elective franchise. In his letter to Thomas Jefferson, he says, "I have abundantly tasted of the fruition of those blessings which proceed from that free and unequalled liberty with which you are favored." All *free men* stood upon equal footing as voters, in Maryland, during the greater part of Banneker's life. There was a property qualification requisite, which, with age and residence, gave the right of voting until 1802. Then the law was changed, and the elective franchise conferred solely upon white men, twenty-one years old, who should have resided a given time in the place of voting. By this change the venerable astronomer was deprived of the valued privilege of voting during the last four years of his life.

We have said that Benjamin Banneker never married, neither did he unite himself with any religious sect. His life was one of constant worship in the great temples of nature and science. In his early days, places of worship were rare. As they increased in number during his later years, he would occasionally visit those of the various denominations. He finally gave a decided preference for the doctrines and form of worship of the Society of Friends, whose meeting-house at Ellicott's Mills he frequently attended.

The author well remembers Banneker's appearance on these occasions, when he always sat on the form nearest the door. He presented a most dignified aspect as he leaned in quiet contemplation on a long staff, which he always carried after passing his seventieth year. "And he worshipped leaning on the top of his staff." His reverent deportment on these occasions added to the natural majesty of his appearance.

The countenance of Banneker had a most benign and thoughtful expression. A fine head of white hair surmounted his unusually broad and ample forehead, whilst the lower part of of his face was slender and sloping towards the chin. His figure was perfectly erect, showing no inclination to stoop as he advanced in years. His raiment was always scrupulously neat; that for summer wear, being of unbleached linen, was beautifully washed and ironed by his sisters, Minta Black and Molly Morton, who we have seen, lived near him, and looked after his domestic affairs. In cold weather he dressed in light colored cloth, a fine drab broadcloth constituting his attire when he designed appearing in his best style.

Being cut off from his favorite employments by reason of his infirmities, and his love of nature remaining ever with him, it so happened that when the great messenger, Death, called for him he was found out upon his favorite hills.

It was on the peaceful Sabbath morning of the 9th of October, 1806, that he strolled forth, as was his custom, to enjoy the air and the sunshine and the view. It was his last look on them with earthly vision. He met an acquaintance, with whom he conversed pleasantly for awhile, when, suddenly complaining of feeling sick, they immediately turned to his cottage. He laid himself upon his couch and never spoke again.   In a little while his mortal frame lay dead.

The following notice of his death is taken from the *Federal Gazette and Baltimore Daily Advertiser,* Tuesday morning, October 28, 1806:

"On Sunday, the 9th instant, departed this life, at his residence in Baltimore County, Mr. Benjamin Banneker, a black man, and immediate descendent of an African father.   He was well known in his neighborhood for his quiet and peaceful demeanor, and, among scientific men, as an astronomer and mathematician.

"In early life he was instructed in the most common rules of arithmetic, and thereafter, with the assistance of different authors, he was enabled to acquire a perfect knowledge of all the higher branches of learning.   Mr. Banneker was the calculator of several almanacs, published in this as well as several of the neighboring States; and, although of late years none of his almanacs have been published, yet he never failed to calculate one every year, and left them among his papers.

"Preferring solitude to mixing with society, he devoted the greater part of his time to reading and contemplation, and to no book was he more attached than the Scriptures.

"At his death, he bequeathed all his astronomical and philosophical books and papers to a friend.

"Mr. Banneker is a prominent instance to prove that a descendent of Africa is susceptible of as great mental improvement and deep knowledge of the mysteries of nature as that of any other nation."

CHAPTER VIII

SOME years prior of Banneker's death, he had been extremely ill, and apprehending that he would not recover, he gave particular directions respecting the disposition of his personal property, but made no written bequests. He ordered that all the articles which had been presented to him by George Ellicott should be returned to him as soon as he should be no more.

It was owing to the singular promptness in carrying out these directions that any souvenirs of this extraordinary man were preserved. On the same day on which he died, one of his nephews carried out his wishes to the letter. Being himself the messenger who conveyed to Ellicott's Mills the tidings of his uncle's death, he arrived at the house of George Ellicott driving a cart, in which was the oval table on which all Banneker's calculations were made; a large number of scientific instruments, and many books on varied topics. These were accompanied by a legacy, which Banneker requested his friend to accept in memory of his long-continued kindness to the giver. It was a large volume of his manuscript and his common-place book. The former volume contains Banneker's observations on various subjects and copies of all his almanacs, as well as copies of his letter to Thomas Jefferson, and the reply of that statesman. We have extracted freely from these books in the preceeding pages.

Banneker left to his surviving sisters, Minta Black and Molly Morton, everything else that he died possessed of. The Bible in which he read seems to have been removed from the house with the same promptness as the legacy to George Ellicott, as it is still extant. His remains were interred two days subsequent to his decease, and whilst the last rites were being performed at his grave, his house took fire, and burned so rapidly that nothing was saved. His clock and all other evidences of his ingenuity and scholarship were consumed in the flames. Some months previous to his death he had given to one of his sisters a feather bed. All his other gifts to her sister and herself, except the Bible, having been destroyed, this bed was highly valued and carefully preserved. After a lapse of some years, she felt something hard among the feathers, which proved to be a purse of money. This simple fact is a pleasing evidence that, though the venerable sage was, through failing health, long hindered from lucrative employment, yet no shadow of poverty rested upon the evening of his honored life.

IN CONCLUSION

WE should in some way show honor to the memory of this wonderful mind, this distinguished citizen, who notwithstanding race prejudice of the times, rose to eminence in scientific attainments. One has only to look at Banneker's picture, "photographed from the original wood-cut," to see a face of determination, "one of intelligence, a face of moral force," under different condition, and different times, a leader of men.

In proposing a NATIONAL BANNEKER MEMORIAL ASSOCIATION, I think it is due him, and I will, in my limited way, use my best efforts to encourage same.

THE AUTHOR.

A Select List of Black Classic Press Titles

The Negro
W. E. B. DuBois

Originally published in 1915, Dr. W. E. Burghardt Du Bois' "little book," as he called it, was one of the most important and seminal works on African and African American history. It was small in size but gigantic in purpose. In it Du Bois, unquestionably an eminent historian, brilliantly attempted to encapsulate the ten thousand-year record of the peoples of Africa, then referred to as "Negroes." Introduction by W. Burghardt Turner and Joyce Moore Turner. ISBN 1-58073-032-9. 1915*, 2005. 281 pp. Paper $14.95.

David Walker's Appeal
David Walker

Walker's Appeal represents one of the earliest African-centered discourses on an oppressed people's right to freedom. African American political philosophy has evolved from many of the themes that it articulates. ISBN 0-933121-38-5. 1929*, 1993. 108 pp. Paper $8.95.

A Tropical Dependency
Flora Shaw Lugard

When Lady Lugard sat down to write *A Tropical Dependency*, it was not her intention to inspire generations of Africans to regain the independence of their countries. Lugard writes of slavery as though it was a God-given right of Europeans to own Africans as slaves. Ironically, her text on Africa's place in history reaffirms the belief that "If Africa did it once, Africa can do it again!" Introduction by John Henrik Clarke. ISBN 0-933121-92-X. 1906*, 1997. 508 pp. Paper $24.95.

The Name "Negro": Its Origin and Evil Use
Richard B. Moore

Moore's study focuses on the exploitive nature of the word "Negro." Connecting its origins to the African Slave Trade, he shows how the label "Negro" was used to separate African descendants and to confirm their supposed inferiority. ISBN 0-933121-35-0. 1960*, 1992. 108 pp. Paper $10.95.

Wonderful Ethiopians of the Ancient Cushite Empire
Drusilla Dunjee Houston

Mrs. Houston describes the origin of civilization and establishes links among the ancient Black populations of Arabia, Persia, Babylonia, and India. In each case, she concludes that the ancient Blacks who inhabited these areas were all culturally related. ISBN 0-933121-01-6. 1926*, 1985. 280 pp. Paper $14.95.

The Exiles of Florida
Joshua R. Giddings
During the early part of the nineteenth century, the United States conducted a brutal campaign to re-enslave Blacks who escaped slavery and found freedom in Native American settlements in Florida. Giddings' observations document the struggle waged by these brave Africans and their Native American hosts.
ISBN 0-933121-47-4. 1858*, 1997. 338 pp. Paper $16.95.

Ancient Egypt the Light of the World
Gerald Massey
An epic analysis of ancient origins and beliefs, this first volume of Ancient Egypt elaborates how the first humans, who emerged in Africa, created thought. In the second volume Massey examines the Precession of the Equinoxes and the old Kamite sources of Christianity.
ISBN 0-933121-31-8. 1907*, 1992. 944 pp. Paper $59.95.

A Book of the Beginnings
Gerald Massey
In volume one, Massey focuses on Egyptian origins in the British Isles. In the second volume, he explores the African/Egyptian roots of the Hebrews, the Akkado-Assyrians, and the Maori. By linking these diverse cultures and origins to their African roots, Massey demonstrates not only the extent of African influence but its durability as well.
ISBN 0-933121-93-8. 1881*, 1995. 1200 pp. Two volume set. Cloth $84.95.

The Natural Genesis
Gerald Massey
By centralizing Egypt as the root of Western civilization's myths, symbols, religions, and languages, this famed Egyptologist and 'mythographer' challenges conventions of theology as well as fundamental notions of race supremacy. Introduction by Dr. Charles S. Finch.
ISBN 1-57478-009-3. 1883*, 1998. 1087 pp. Two volume set. Paper $59.95.

Christianity, Islam and the Negro Race
Edward W. Blyden
Blyden offers an early African-centered perspective on race, religion, and the development of Africa.
ISBN 0-933121-41-5. 1887*, 1993. 441 pp. Paper $14.95.

To order, send a check or money order to:
Black Classic Press
P.O. Box 13414-b
Baltimore, MD 21203-3414

Include $5 for shipping and handling, and $.50 for each additional book ordered.
Credit card orders call: 1-800-476-8870

For a complete list of titles, please visit our website at www.blackclassic.com

Indicates first year published

100119-150-13-60W